YOU CAN PLAY CRICKET

Bowling, batting, fielding techniques;
games to improve skill and control;
history, rules and regulations;
umpire's signals and a useful glossary of terms.

Whether you wish to improve your game
or have never played before, this
excellent handbook is a thorough introduction
and aid for the young cricketer, presented
in a practical and lively way by that
great cricketer and former England Captain,
Tex Dexter.

Other titles in the YOU CAN series include:

YOU CAN SWIM
YOU CAN BE A GYMNAST
YOU CAN PLAY FOOTBALL

Published by Carousel Books

YOU CAN PLAY CRICKET

A CAROUSEL BOOK 0 552 54199 0

First published in Great Britain by
Carousel Books

PRINTING HISTORY

Carousel edition published 1982

Text Copyright © Victorama Ltd. 1982
Illustrations copyright © Mike Miller 1982

Carousel Books are published by
Transworld Publishers Ltd.,
Century House, 61–63 Uxbridge Road,
Ealing, London, W5 5SA

Made and printed by The Guernsey Press Co. Ltd.,
Guernsey, Channel Islands.

You Can Play Cricket

Ted Dexter

Illustrated by Mike Miller

CAROUSEL BOOKS

A DIVISION OF TRANSWORLD PUBLISHERS LTD

Contents

INTRODUCTION

I first became interested in cricket at a very early age, when, like many young boys, I received a cricket bat from my parents as a present. Perhaps if they had given me a football instead my life might have been totally different, but as it was they gave me a bat and I played my very first game of cricket, completely unaware of the future that lay ahead of me.

I can remember that first bat very clearly indeed, not merely because of the enjoyment it brought, but because on one occasion in a particularly boisterous game of cricket with my brother I got hit straight between the eyes with it and still bear the scar to this very day! I hasten to add that it was purely accidental and my brother had no intention of hitting me! That incident taught me that however enjoyable a sport may be, there is always an element of danger and a chance that you might get hurt, and so in cricket especially it is important to have proper protection and padding.

Whilst still a lad I remember playing 'Tip-and-Run' with the W.A.A.F., a game in which I was uncertain what I should do, and recall crying my eyes out because after having hit the ball I didn't realise that you had to run! Again, I learnt a valuable lesson and that is to make quite certain you fully understand the rules of any game you are going to play, so that you know exactly what to do.

Later I played compulsory cricket for my school, and it was at that time I realised that being a professional cricketer was what I really wanted to do. After a lot of hard work I achieved this aim and eventually experienced something that every cricketer longs for — I became captain of the English cricket team.

It was as Captain that one of the greatest moments in my career took place. That was in the 1962/63 England-Australia Test Series when we beat Australia at Melbourne and brought back the 'Ashes' to England. It was not until after the match that it actually dawned upon me that we had beaten them and I was Captain. It was a wonderful and unforgettable moment.

Of course, there are disappointing moments too. Probably the most regrettable moment of my life was the point when I suddenly realised that I was getting old and that my reflexes were not as good as they used to be. But I still love the game as much as ever, and one can still gain great pleasure from watching other people take an active part.

If you enjoy cricket, or even if you have never played before, I hope that this book will help you find out more about the game and enjoy it to the full. I have tried to explain as simply as possible the rules of the game, what you need to know to be a good cricketer, how the game began, and a look at some of the greatest cricketers there have ever been.

The best advice I can give you is to remember that cricket is an intricate and many sided game, and you are never too old to learn. A cricketer goes on learning new skills all his life, and no cricketer is ever too good to stop learning. So, remember to keep learning all the time, enjoy your game, and if your parents have given you a bat, just as mine did, who knows . . . you too might one day have the honour of being cricket Captain for England.

Ted Dexter

THE HISTORY OF CRICKET

A cricket match today is played between two sides of 11 players. They play on a cricket field, in the centre of which is a smooth strip called the **pitch**. The pitch is normally 22 yards (20.12 m) long, though it can be shorter for younger players.

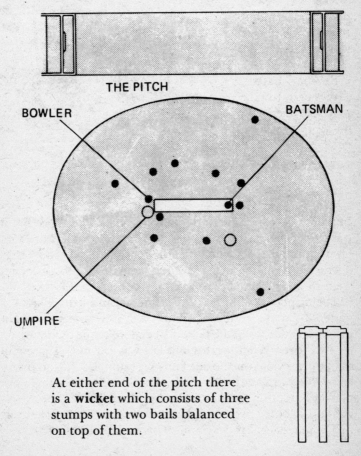

THE PITCH

BOWLER

BATSMAN

UMPIRE

At either end of the pitch there is a **wicket** which consists of three stumps with two bails balanced on top of them.

Apart from a few changes, cricket has been played on pitches like this for the past two hundred years. But the game itself is much older than that.

The name **wicket** means a small gate, and it is possible that the earliest form of cricket was a game played by shepherds bowling a ball at a wicket gate while one man defended the gate with a bat. Later games used to take place between sides made up of whole villages.

In fact cricket became so popular in the Middle Ages that it was one of the pastimes banned by King Edward III in 1365. He disapproved of cricket, and the other games, because they distracted people from their work so much. This ban does not seem to have been very successful however, and cricket was still being played a hundred years later when a stricter law was passed to make it illegal. This said that anyone caught playing cricket would be fined £10 and would be put in prison for two years. Whether this new law was any more successful than the previous one no one knows for sure, but historians do know that pupils at the free school in Guildford, Surrey, were playing what they called **creckett** in about 1550. However, it was still another two and a half centuries before cricket was finally made legal in England. This took place in 1784.

Cricket was being openly played long before this date and the laws preventing the game seem to have been completely forgotten. Cricket matches became very popular among the wealthy men in the country. Lords, Dukes and other aristocrats used to bet large sums of money on cricket matches, in the hope that their own sides would win, and that they would win all the money that had been bet.

The first county match was also played long before 1784. This took place in 1719 at a site in London called Lamb's Conduit Fields, when the Kent county side played a side representing London.

However, cricket as we know it today really began in Hampshire sometime in the 1760's, when the village of Hambledon formed its own cricket club. Although the players were only local farmers and small businessmen, like their captain, Robert Nyren, who was the landlord of the *Bat and Ball Inn* on Broadhalfpenny Down, they beat the best sides in England — and they created many of the techniques of cricket which still apply more than two hundred years later.

One of the best eighteenth century cricketers was a Yorkshire-man named **Thomas Lord**. His name is remembered today for **Lord's cricket ground**, the most famous in the world, which he founded. Thomas Lord actually opened his first ground in Dorset Square, in London, at the time when Middlesex played Essex in 1787. He later moved to a second site, in Regent's Park, before finally moving to the area of London called St. John's Wood, where Lord's has remained ever since.

Lord's has become particularly famous in the cricket world, because it has been the home of the Marylebone Cricket Club, the **M.C.C.**, since the end of the eighteenth century. The M.C.C. has played a leading part in the history of cricket, one of its most important actions being in 1835, when it drew up a revised set of laws for the game, many of which still govern cricket today.

During the nineteenth century cricket spread throughout the British Empire to countries as far apart as Australia, the West Indies, New Zealand, South Africa and India. In 1859 an English touring side went abroad for the first time. However, it did not play against countries which we think of as being great cricket centres today. It went on a tour of North America to play sides in Canada and the U.S.A. instead. Back at home the county championship began in England in 1873 with 9 counties taking part; today the number has increased to 17. Then, four years later in 1877, came the first **Test match**.

A Test match is a game played between two countries. This first one took place between Australia and England, and it was played in the Australian city of Melbourne. Alfred Shaw opened the bowling for England and the Australian batsman, Charles Bannerman, scored the first run. Bannerman went on to score 165, the first Test century, and he might have scored even more runs if he had not had to retire from his innings hurt. However, Australia won the match by 45 runs. By a curious coincidence history repeated itself in the centenary match that was played between England and Australia in Melbourne in 1977. As in the first Test, a hundred years before, Australia beat England by 45 runs, exactly the same winning margin.

Over 850 Test matches have been played since that first one in Melbourne. Tests have been played between all the major cricketing countries in New Zealand, the West Indies, Pakistan, India, South Africa and England, as well as in Australia.

To begin with Test matches were only played between England, Australia and South Africa, but between the two world wars the programme widened. The West Indies joined in 1928, New Zealand the next season and India was the last in 1932 (Pakistan was part of India until 1947). However, the administrative centre of the game remained in London, at Lord's. In 1947 the M.C.C. revised the laws for a second time and with their amendments, these have controlled every game of cricket in the world ever since.

However, as cricket moved into the 1960's other changes were on the way. In 1963 the old distinction between amateur and professional players in English first class cricket disappeared. From then on all players were simply called **cricketers**, although there was nothing to prevent them from being paid by the counties for whom they played. In 1968 the Cricket Council was formed to take over most of the control of English cricket from the M.C.C. and the Test and County Cricket Board took over the organization of Test series and the important job of developing county cricket. 1968 also saw an important change in the rules which allowed English counties to include one overseas player in their sides without having to wait for him to be registered as living in England.

But probably the biggest changes in cricket were brought about after the **Packer affair**. In May 1977, Kerry Packer, an Australian television businessman, announced that he was going to stage a series of matches in which Australia would play sides made up from over thirty of the world's best players from other countries. As a result these players were prevented from playing for many of their national sides, but the large earnings they made from the Packer cricket **circus** brought pay rises to other top cricketers, who had always earned far less than footballers and other professional sportsmen. The trouble caused by the Packer affair has died down now, but cricket will never be the same again.

Apart from the increased earnings for players, it also introduced cricket played at night with a white ball and players wearing black pads. Happily a lot of the Packer players have been allowed to return to play for their countries again.

THE FIELD

Cricket fields today have developed a long way from the mediaeval meadows where the game began. Wherever grass grows cricket fields are carefully mown, level, open spaces, and the most important ones are surrounded by seats for spectators. The field itself can be any size and shape, but the playing area should be contained within a **boundary** line that is at least 75 yards (73 m) from the pitch.

The game is concentrated on and around the **pitch**. Here the surface is as smooth and level as possible, and its condition plays a very important part in the game. Players will spend a long time examining the pitch to see how worn it is and how wet, or dry, it is. When it rains the pitch is the only part of the ground to be covered with screens and if the pitch is deliberately damaged, as happened in one Test match not so long ago, the game is often abandoned.

The **stumps**, at either end of the pitch, are stuck into the ground along a line called the **bowling crease**. Today the wicket formed by these three stumps is 28½ inches (71.12 cm) high and 9 inches (22.86 cm) wide. Until 1776 however, there were only two stumps in a wicket and these supported one long **bail**.

The bowling crease is 8 feet 8 inches (2.64 m) long and the wicket stands right in the middle of it. Four feet (1.22 m) in front of the bowling crease is another line called the **popping crease**, which is at least 12 feet (3.66 m) long. The popping crease is important for batsmen, between that line and the bowling crease they are safe, but outside it they run the risk of getting out.

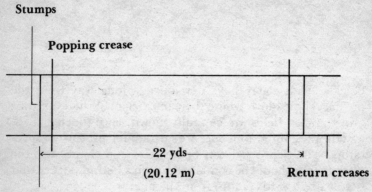

Running on either side of the bowling crease are two other lines called the **return** creases. These stretch from the popping crease back past the bowling crease for a distance of **again** at least 4 feet (1.22 m).

So if you could look at the pitch from above you would see two **H shapes** with slightly longer lines at their tops pointing **towards each** other down a smooth carpet of grass. And if you **walked out** to measure the pitch the distance from one **bowling crease** to the other should be — yes, you've got it — 22 yards (20.12 m).

One other thing which you might notice on the field are two large white screens standing outside the boundary. These are called **sightscreens** and they are built on little wheels so that they can be moved from side to side in a line with the pitch.

They are there to help the batsmen see the ball when it is bowled. On some dull days and against some backgrounds the small red ball can be difficult to see. The large white screen behind the bowler's arm makes it easier for the batsman to see it coming — this can be very important with a ball travelling at nearly 100 m.p.h. (160 km/h)!

THE GAME

In a nutshell the object of a game of cricket is to score more **runs** than the other side, just as in football the object is to score more goals. But whereas in football both sides try to score goals at the same time, in cricket they take it in turns — and these turns are called **innings**.

Before a match begins the captains of the two sides toss a coin. The winner of the toss can then decide whether his side will bat first and have their innings (or in the case of a two-innings match their first innings), or whether he will put the other side into bat first. This decision is taken with great care. The weather, the condition of the pitch, the condition of the players and his opinion of the other side all have to be taken into consideration. It is much more complicated than simply winning the kick-off in football or rugby.

Once the decision is made the game gets under way. All but two of the players of the side put in to bat stay off the field, the players of the other side walk on to take the field first, and because of this they are known as the **fielding side**.

Only one of them has a set position on the field. That is the **wicket-keeper**, who as his name suggests positions himself behind the wicket at one end of the pitch. This is the end where the first **batsman** will begin his side's innings.

The captain of the fielding side then chooses his **bowler** to open the game from among the remaining ten players. And finally he and the bowler between them tell the other players where on the field they should stand as **fielders**. (The section on **Fielding** explains these positions).

Meanwhile the first two batsmen of the batting side come onto the field to open their innings. The **batting order** of each side is decided by the captain and the best batsmen usually go in to bat early on. One batsman goes to the end of the wicket where the wicket-keeper is standing. He is the **striker** and will receive the first ball from the bowler, who bowls from the other end of the pitch, where the other batsman (the **non-striker**) stands behind the popping crease.

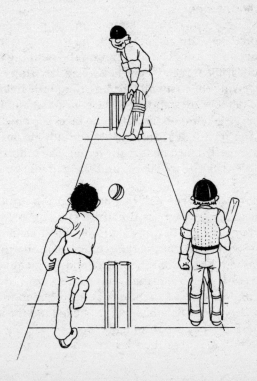

The field now has thirteen players. But there are two other men standing on it as well. They are the **umpires** who control the game and make sure that the rules are followed. (The section on **Umpires** explains what they do and where they stand).

Every time a batsman comes to the wicket to bat he is allowed to ask the umpire at the bowling end for a **guard**. This is the position which he takes up in front of the wicket so that he can best defend the stumps. To take his guard he stands holding the bat straight up, with its bottom on the popping crease. The umpire then directs him to the guard he has asked for and the batsman usually marks this on the popping crease so that he does not forget where it is. The last thing he does before receiving the first ball is to look round the field and see where the fielders are standing. If he is a right-hand batsman the side of the ground on his left, as he faces the bowling end, is called the **on** (or **leg**) side, while the side on his right is known as the **off**. Once he is ready to bat, the umpire signals to the bowler that he may bowl and the game begins.

The bowler delivers the ball by hand according to the rules explained in the section on **Bowling**. His aim is to get the batsman out through bowling skilfully. The batsman has to defend the wicket and at the same time use his bat to hit the ball far enough away from the wicket and the fielders to give himself, and the other batsman, time to run down the pitch, from one popping crease to the one at the other end. In order to do this safely both batsmen have to be behind the popping creases to which they are running before the fielding side can return the ball to one of the wickets and knock off the bails.

Whenever the batsmen succeed in running between the wickets they score a run. If they run twice, they score two runs. And sometimes with very long hits they have time to run between the wicket three times to score three runs. When the ball goes over the boundary though there is no need for the batsmen to run. **If a ball goes over the boundary but touches the ground before it does, then four runs are added to the score. If it sails over without touching the ground at all, six runs are added**. In the cases where the batsmen hit the ball to score, the runs are added to their personal scores, which together make up the score of the side. However, runs can also be scored by **extras** and these are simply added to the side's total at the end of the innings.

Extras are awarded for three reasons. When the umpire calls a **no ball** after a bowler breaks one of the rules of bowling. When the umpire calls a **wide** if he thinks that the ball was bowled too far for the batsman to be able to reach it. And for a **bye** when the batsman misses the ball, or lets it pass and the wicket-keeper fails to stop it. In this case, and also if the wicket-keeper fails to stop a wide, the batsmen can run as many runs as they think safe. What's more, if the ball passes over the boundary, four byes are awarded.

Each bowler bowls a series of six balls (eight in Australia) from one end. This series is called an **over**. When each over is finished, the fielding side changes ends and the next bowler delivers his over from the other wicket. Even if two bowlers do most of the bowling for their side, they still bowl alternate overs with the field changing ends between each.

When one batsman is out the next one in the batting order comes to the wicket to take his place. This continues until all the batsmen in the batting side have had an innings and ten of them have been out. When the last man is out, the innings is finished and the fielding side have their turn to bat in their first innings.

GEAR AND CLOTHING

Cricket equipment has changed only a little in the last two hundred years.

The modern **cricket ball** is made from a cork and twine core covered with a red leather casing. It must weigh between 5½ and 5¾ ounces (156−163 g.) and it has to measure between 8 13/16 and 9 inches (22.38 − 22.86 cm) in circumference. It has a seam around its centre which is important for many types of bowling.

The cricket **bat** has changed more in shape over the centuries than the ball. Originally cricket bats were shaped more like hockey sticks.

But the modern shape began to develop from the end of the 18th century, with a straight-sided face and a bulge at the back near the bottom (the **toe**). Most cricket bats are carved from white willow wood and the handles are made from cane and thin layers of rubber, bound with twine and covered with a rubber sleeve. No bat can be more than 38 inches (96.52 cm) long and 4¼ inches (10.80 cm) wide.

The usual clothing for cricket is a pair of white, or cream trousers, a shirt of the same colour, a white pullover, with or without sleeves, white boots, with some sort of spikes and a cap, if it's very sunny.

Wicket keepers and batsmen need additional protective clothing.

On their legs they wear pads which protect them from their ankles to their thighs. On their hands they wear padded gloves with fingers. They wear a special guard to protect their groin, and in some recent Test matches batsmen have worn helmets too, though these are not common yet among county players.

TOURNAMENTS

In England the major competition for county sides is the **Schweppes County Championship**.

This is a competition in which the 17 English counties with first class cricket sides play each other in three-day matches throughout the summer. However, the demand for faster, more exciting cricket led to three major competitions in which the sides only batted for a limited number of overs. This led to a new, fast scoring, daring running type of cricket, which has become very popular in England, but less so in other countries.

Schtumped!

The competition with the shortest number of overs is the **John Player League**. These matches have only 40 overs and are always played on Sundays. The competition began in 1969 for the 17 major counties, which play eight home games and eight away games during the season. At the end of the season the champions receive a trophy and £1,000, while the runners-up win £500. There are also prizes for individual players. Every hit for six is rewarded, so is the taking of four wickets in an innings.

The Benson and Hedges Cup includes two Minor County sides and a side from Oxford and Cambridge, as well as the 17 first class sides. The sides play in four leagues, with the top two from each going forward to a knock-out competition, with a final at Lord's in July. The winners receive a gold trophy and a cash prize, but there are also awards for best player in each match.

The longest matches in a limited over competition are in the **Natwest Trophy**, in which each side bats for 60 overs. This competition began in 1963 and as well as the 17 first class county sides, the top five sides from the Minor Counties also take part. The competition works on a knock-out basis and it has one interesting rule that differs from normal cricket. In the Natwest Trophy no bowler may bowl more than twelve overs.

WORLD COMPETITIONS

The most important world competitions are the **Test series** played between the leading cricket countries. Matches in a Test series usually last for five days and these give players an opportunity to make high scores and test their ability against the toughest competition. Test matches can also be fascinating battles of wits between rival captains, especially in England, where the weather can be very unpredictable and can alter the whole course of a game with a sudden downpour of rain.

The **Prudential World Cup** offers a chance for all the cricket playing countries to compete in one competition and for the two finalists to play the deciding match at Lord's.

As well as these international competitions, first class sides around the world compete in their own national competitions. In Australia the principal competition is the **Sheffield Shield** in which all the states play each other twice a season in matches that last three days, to decide which is the winner. There is also a one-day cricket competition called the **McDonald Cup**.

In nearby New Zealand the equivalent of the Schweppes County Championship is the **Plunket Shield**, which is competed for by the four major provinces — Auckland, Canterbury, Otago and Wellington, as well as sides from the Central District and Northern Districts.

Nowhere is cricket more popular than in India and Pakistan. Thousands of Indians attend matches between state sides in the **Ranji Trophy**, the **Duleep Trophy**, the **Irani Trophy** and others. While over the border in Pakistan first class sides compete in the **Quaid-I-Azam Trophy** and the **Ayub Zonal Trophy**.

Strangely enough the West Indies, which has produced so many winning Test sides did not have a first class inter-island competition until the introduction of the **Shell Shield** in the mid-1960's. And although the Caribbean is the centre of cricket in the western hemisphere, it is easy to forget that there are cricket competitions played in the United States and Canada as well. These may be nothing like the competitions in other countries, but it's worth remembering that the first international match ever played took place between these two countries.

The other major cricket country, South Africa, has not featured in world sport for several years. However, there are some excellent sides in the country and they compete against each other in the **Currie Cup**, one of the oldest cricket competitions in the world, which was founded in 1890.

FIELDING

Since every cricketer should expect to spend more time fielding in a cricket match than doing anything else it's not only important to know how to field well, but also to know how to enjoy fielding.

No matter where in the field you are positioned the most important rule to remember is to watch the ball all the time. If you are fielding close to the wicket you will have to be on the look-out for fast, difficult catches off the bat. If you are further out in the field you will have to watch the direction of the ball as it leaves the bat and intercept it as quickly as you can.

Fielding often seems dull and unexciting and it can easily become this if you let it. However, if a whole field of fielders are on their toes waiting eagerly for a **catch**, or **a run-out** from a piece of quick fielding, the game develops into a fascinating battle of wits between the batsmen and the fielders.

The fielder's aim in any match must be to be quick and tidy in his fielding. He must learn to retrieve the ball cleanly, and not to let it slip out of his grasp. He must learn to throw it accurately to the wicket, even when he's in a rush to get a run-out. And he must learn to catch any ball cleanly and with confidence.

One well saved ball may not necessarily win a match, but it may make a batsman more cautious next time, and prevent him scoring runs. And one dropped catch may not lose a match, but one caught catch means another dismissal and gives a greater chance of winning.

Fielding Positions

If you forget about the bowler and the wicket-keeper, there are only 9 fielders on the field during a match. Where they stand is a matter for the captain and the bowler to decide. If they want an **attacking field**, the fielders will be grouped close to the wicket. If they want a more **spread out field**, the fielders will be nearer the boundary. Every position on the field has its name and every cricketer is expected to know where each one is. This diagram will help find your place when the captain tells you to stand at Silly Mid Off, or Deep Extra Cover for example. These positions are those taken up for a right-handed batsman. If the batsman is left-handed, the positions are on the other side of the pitch.

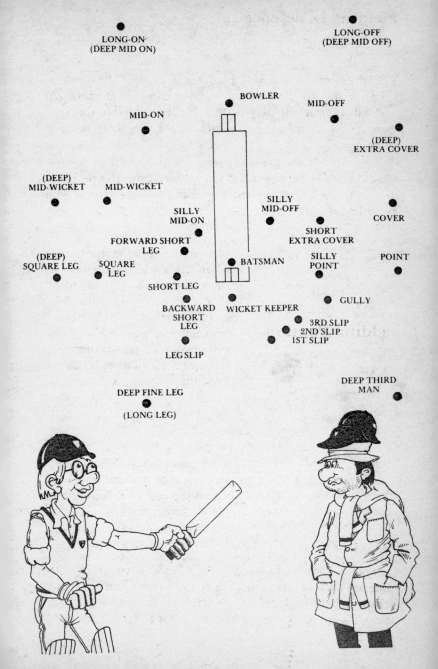

Fielding in defence

The object of the defensive fielder is to prevent the batsmen from scoring runs. This requires just as much concentration and skill as attacking play as any mistakes mean that the batsmen can score more runs, which could win their side the game.

Most defensive fielding takes place away from the positions nearest to the bat. So it is usually fielders in the out-field who are called on to do this.

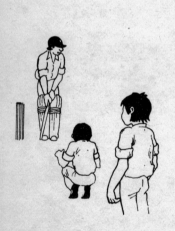

Starting from the moment when the bowler approaches the wicket to bowl, the fielders should all begin to walk in towards the wicket. This will get them 'on the move' and will make it easier for them to move to the ball after it has been hit.

They must watch the ball onto the bat and then watch the direction in which the batsman hits it.

Every out-fielder has a section of the field to defend, but this must not prevent others running round to back him up. If one fielder fails to stop the ball, a back-up fielder can at least prevent it running over the boundary for four.

When a hard drive heads out towards a fielder, the fielder has to position himself to stop this cleanly. Not only must he run to the right place to intercept the ball, but he must be sure too that his body is behind the ball, so that it forms a complete barrier.

The best way of doing this is to turn sideways to the line of the ball and go down on your left knee, so that it comes up against the heel of your right boot. If you keep your hands and head low, your body will now be a large barrier at right angles to the ball and will certainly stop it passing through your defence.

Once you have gathered the ball cleanly, you will be able to throw it back to the wicket, cleanly and effectively, having saved four runs.

Fielding in attack

The attacking fielder stops runs, like the defending fielder, but he also tries to help the bowler and the wicket-keeper to dismiss the batsmen.

He does everything the defending fielder does, but it is done quicker and with greater urgency. Clearly the best policy is to attack whenever possible. This way you can unsettle the batsmen and possibly force them to make mistakes, and so get themselves out.

So watch the ball from the moment just before it is bowled, try to anticipate from the shot where in the field it has been hit and then run to intercept this as soon as you can, if it is in your sector. Run all the same, even if another fielder is going to stop it. You can help by running behind to back him up.

When you reach the ball it will still probably be moving fast across the ground. Try to swoop down on it and gather it with your hands, just as it comes alongside your right foot, which will provide a barrier if you miss.

It will also mean that your weight will be on your right foot, and you will be in a good position to throw the ball to the wicket.

All you have to do is shift your weight to your left leg, which is pointed at the wicket, and as you do so throw the ball to the wicket-keeper's gloves, or to the fielder at the bowler's end.

A piece of fielding like this is often unseen, and unexpected by the batsmen. They may be trying to take another run as you turn to throw the ball. See which batsman is furthest from his wicket and throw to that wicket. If there is nothing between them, throw to the wicket-keeper, who stands a better chance of catching a long, hard throw. **Aim to throw the ball so that it arrives just above the bails**. A good throw could make the difference between a run-out and a wasted chance.

If you are closer to the wicket, you can risk trying to gather the ball with one hand and throwing it, all in one movement. This is well worth practising for those chances you might have of throwing the ball at the wicket yourself to get a quick run-out.

So you should try to be an attacking fielder with poor shots, and those that you can intercept. But the good, hard shots that either come straight towards you, or which have to be stopped at all costs, call for careful defensive fielding.

Catching

No matter where you stand in the field, close to the bat, in the out-field, behind the bat, in front of the bat, you will always have the chance of taking a catch, and this above all else requires total concentration on the ball.

Catching close to the bat is dealt with next, so let's just deal with the **out-fielder** here. Catches in the out-field come from miss-hit shots that the batsman intended to go over the boundary, so they are usually high. Assuming that you have started to move in as the bowler runs up, the first thing you must do when the ball sails into the air is to judge its flight. And you must do this standing still. Do not move until you are certain of the direction in which it is heading. Once you have made up your mind, get onto the line of flight as fast as you can. Don't run into other players who might stand a better chance of catching it. But if you are certain that yours is the best chance don't be afraid to shout *Mine*, to stop them running into you.

Try to get underneath the ball and stand still as it comes to you. Keep your head still and watch the ball all the way. As soon as you are underneath it, cup your hands, with the fingers pointing up. Take the catch just above eye-level, close your fingers round the ball as soon as it is in your hands safely, and then let your arms and hands give naturally to take the catch in front of your chest.

Think of the ball as a raw egg, which you don't want to break. This will help you catch it securely, but gently. And it will stop you trying to snatch at the ball, and risk dropping it.

If the ball comes at you directly on a line with your head, you should hold your hands in a different way.

Hold them with the thumbs touching and the fingers pointing up, so that the ball can fly into them, just to one side of your head.

Then as soon as it's in your hands, close your fingers round it to prevent it popping out, and let your hands and arms give with the force of the catch.

Above all catches should be relaxed and yielding. They run a great risk of being dropped if they are taken hastily, or if you are off balance. So be still and watch the ball into your hands.

Fielding close to the wicket

Whereas fielders in the out-field see the ball coming to them, fielders close to the wicket make catches by instinct and move by reflex action — they seldom see the ball coming to them.

So fielders standing in the **slips**, or at **gully**, **short leg**, or **silly mid-off**, have to be very quick on their toes and have to concentrate on every delivery as if it was going to give them a certain catch.

While out-fielders start to move in as the bowler runs up, the fielders close to the wicket have to be in position before he starts to run in. The correct position for all close fielders is a **low** one, which allows them to spring in any direction or drop even lower if they have to.

Before the bowler starts his run, therefore, the close fielders should get into a comfortable crouching position. Their weight should be evenly placed on both feet, so that they can spring off one or the other. Their knees should be bent and their bottoms should be down near the ground. They should hold their hands ready for a catch with the palms pointing towards a likely catch and the fingers pointing towards the ground. But the great secret of close-fielding is to stay like this until the ball has left the bat. If you get up too soon, you might miss the low ball. Get down, watch the ball, keep your head still and then spring to the catch when you hear the **snick** off the edge of the bat. If you can, try to watch the ball into your hands, but in any case let your hands give, so that it does not bounce out.

FIELDING GAMES

The simplest fielding games are the ones that you can play on your own, when you've got even a few minutes to spare. If you have a golf ball, or a tennis ball, throw it against a concrete wall and catch it and stop it as it comes off the wall at different heights.

If you have an open space near your wall, stick a stump or a piece of wood in the ground and when your ball comes back at you off the wall, take it cleanly and try to throw it at the stump and knock it over.

If there are two of you, you can both have a ball and try to be the first to knock over the stump. On the other hand you can use one ball and take it in turns to throw it at the wall, so that the other player has to catch it. Mark a line parallel to the wall on the ground, but three metres from it. Decide that the ball must come back off the wall and land at least three metres from the wall (ie. on your side of the line). Then take it in turns to throw the ball so that it gives the other player difficult catches. Every catch you take gives you a point. The first player to get to nine wins.

High Ball

This is a catching game for five or more players. One player stands in the centre of a circle formed by the others. The players in the circle either stand with their backs to the one in the middle, or else they face him, but with their eyes closed. Before the game begins, the players are each given a number. Then they take up their positions and the player in the centre throws the ball into the air, or if he can, hits it into the air with a cricket bat. As he does so he calls out: 'Yours Number. . .' The player whose number has been called, then spins round, or opens his eyes, finds where the ball is and then moves into position to catch it cleanly. The first player to take five successful catches, goes into the middle, and so on.

Bucket Ball

This is a running, fielding and throwing game. To play it you need a cricket bat, a ball, a bucket and a chair, as well as at least five players, the more the better.

One player takes the bat and stands near the bucket, which is placed on its side, on the chair — this is the target. Another player takes the ball, and stands near the batsman. The other players then line up about 30 metres away from the target.

The player with the ball then throws it up for the batsman to hit, while the first player in the line starts to move in. As soon as the ball is hit, he has to race after it, field it and then throw it into the bucket. Meanwhile the **bowler** moves behind the bucket and becomes the **wicket-keeper**.

If the ball is thrown into the bucket the fielder gets 10 points. But if it misses and the wicket-keeper has to move away to stop it, the fielder loses one point for every pace the wicket-keeper takes. So a move of four paces is 4 minus points. After each turn the fielder goes to the back of the line. After ten turns the game ends. The highest total wins and that fielder becomes the next batsman, second highest is the bowler.

BATTING

First and foremost a batsman must aim to help his side win. He may do this by scoring a high total himself, but he might equally do it by playing a sensible, controlled game at one end of the pitch, while the more experienced batsmen hit high scores at the other. Batting is not always an opportunity to win a game single-handed, although many players like to look at it in that way. A good batsman should look for runs whenever he can make them, but he should also know when to get his head down and play a controlled, measured game.

At the wicket the batsman is very much on his own. He will always have the wicket-keeper behind him waiting to snap up any careless shots, and he may often have a group of fielders gathered round in a tight circle. So batting always needs great concentration. But it must be concentration on each ball as it is bowled. If you play a bad shot on one ball and get away with it, don't brood over that for the rest of the over. Put it out of your mind before the next delivery and make a mental note to think a little harder.

Before you even start to play shots though, give yourself a big advantage and learn to hold the bat correctly. You can do this quite simply by laying the bat face down on the ground in front of you and then picking it up as if you were going to lift it above your head to use as a chopper. This grip should be relaxed but firm. Check that your hands are close together and that they are towards the top of the handle.

How to stand

When you come to the wicket for the first time you need to know where you are standing in relation to the wicket and the bowler who is trying to hit it. To help you stand in the correct place you take what is called your **guard**. This is a position which you mark on the crease, so that you can always stand with your legs just outside the stumps, your bat in front of them and your head directly over the middle stump. This helps you defend your wicket and judge your shots correctly. The umpire will direct you to move your bat to the correct position for the guard you have chosen and you can then make a small mark to remember it by. The most usual guards are **leg stump**, **middle stump** and half-way between these, **middle and leg**. After some practice you will find out which one suits you best.

Leg stump

Middle and
leg stump

Middle stump

The next thing to get right is the way you stand when you are batting. **Remember that cricket is a sideways game**. By this we mean that whether you are batting, bowling or throwing in from the field, you are pointing your left shoulder (if you are right-handed) towards the bowler, the batsman, or the wicket.

So when you are batting stand with the bottom of your bat behind your feet. Your feet should be set apart, on either side of the popping crease. You should place your weight evenly on both of them. Turn your left shoulder towards the bowler and turn your head so that you can look at the bowler's hand. Never take your eyes off the ball. Watch it all the way to the bat.

Backlift

Every cricket stroke should begin with the backlift. This is the movement that the batsman makes as the bowler is about to bowl the ball. Without a good backlift it is very difficult to play a solid straight bat to the ball, and, as we'll see, a straight bat is essential to good batting.

The secret of the backlift is to lift the bat straight back using wrists and arms only. The head and the body should be kept perfectly still, so that the batsman can keep his eyes fixed on the ball all the time.

If he moves his head, he can easily lose sight of the ball. If this happens only for a fraction of a second it can make the difference between playing a safe stroke and being bowled or caught out.

You should aim to lift the bat back to a height where the middle of the bat is level with your eyes. Practise this in front of a mirror where you can watch that your backlift is both straight and high. Check too that your head and body can remain quite still while you do it.

Forward defensive shot

The forward defensive shot is the basic shot on which all forward strokes in cricket are based. It is used to block a ball which is well pitched up and bowled with a good line towards the wicket.

The aim of the shot is to stop the ball, it is not a shot off which you would expect to score any runs, let alone a six.

To play the forward defensive shot you move your front foot forward so that you tread alongside the ball as it pitches. Your back foot keeps still, your left (forward) knee should be slightly bent, and you must aim to bring your bat straight down and very close to this knee and alongside your left (forward) foot. Timing this stroke is very important. Make sure that you hit the ball with the middle of the bat. To do this you'll have to keep your head down and watch the ball right onto the bat. You have to be careful too that the ball does not fly up in the air, and give a catch. But you can avoid this happening by getting your head right over the ball and stopping the bat just in front of your front foot. Do this and the ball will drop dead in front of you. Again a straight bat is very important, so practise in front of a mirror until you can move smoothly into the shot.

Forward attacking shot

In the forward defensive shot the batsman really does nothing except put the bat in the way of the ball, so that it hits up against it. In the forward attacking shot the movements are essentially the same. The difference being that with the attacking shot the batsman aims to hit the ball with the full swing of the bat.

You can play forward attacking shots off balls which are over-pitched and which you can easily reach when you go forward. Go through the motions of the forward defensive shot, that is high backlift, front foot forward alongside the ball when it pitches, straight bat coming down beside the forward knee and hitting the ball in the middle of the bat. But now, instead of stopping the bat by your foot, allow it to go through the line of the ball, hitting it hard as you do. Then continue the stroke with a straight follow through which will bring the bat up and over your left shoulder.

It's the follow through that sends the ball, just as it does in any ball game from tennis to golf. Make sure with the follow through that you keep your left elbow up, don't let it droop down into your side. If you do you will hit the ball with a cross bat and may miss it completely. The forward attacking shot must be hit with a straight bat every time.

Again you can practise your line in front of a mirror, though if you can persuade someone to lob a ball at you, this will give you the real thing to hit.

Body position for a short pitched ball

If a ball pitches short, that is if you cannot reach it comfortably by playing forward, then you must go back. Don't be undecided about it. Look at the flight of the ball, judge where it will pitch and if you see that it is going to be too far from you, don't wave your bat at it, and so give away catches, keep a straight bat, get in line with the ball and watch it carefully onto the bat.

With most short pitched balls you will need to step back. This can work to your advantage though, because it gives just a little longer to look at the ball and so judge your shot. There are defensive strokes and attacking strokes which you can play off the back foot, just as there are ones off the front foot. The main thing to remember is that you must get your head over the ball and your body behind it when you go back. Whether you are hitting a short-pitched ball with an attacking shot, or whether you are aiming to drop it dead at your feet, you must be positive in your movements and controlled in your play.

Quite often you will be faced with short pitched balls from pace bowlers. These can rise off the pitch and come flying at you at frightening speeds sometimes. But once you have acquired the confidence to get behind the line of the ball and play it with a straight bat, your fear will disappear. And as with every other stroke, the success of doing this lies in watching the ball all the time.

Back defensive shot

When you can't comfortably reach a ball that pitches on a length by moving forwards to stop it, you have to play back to it.

The same rules apply to this back defensive shot as applied to the forward defensive one, the only difference being that you step back with your back foot, instead of stepping forward with your front foot.

Once you've made your mind to play a back defensive stroke, the first thing you must do is to step back about half-way to the stumps, placing your back foot in line with the spot where the ball bounces. Keep all your weight on this back foot, so that your front foot just touches the ground. Your front leg should be parallel to the popping crease.

Try to tilt your body and head slightly forward as you play the shot, keeping your left elbow well up so that the bat will be perfectly straight as it comes through beside your forward leg.

As with the forward defensive shot, don't be tempted to push out at the ball, let it come through to the bat. In this way it will drop dead at your toes even if it has moved after pitching, providing the bat points slightly towards the ground. Let it point up the other way and you'll give an easy catch.

Back attacking shot

The motions of this shot are similar to those of the back defensive shot.

This shot is used for forcing balls that are shorter pitched than the ones to which you would play forward. As with the back defensive shot the batsman should step back with his back foot in line with the ball. He should put all his weight on that back foot and will have to use all his height, maybe even getting up on his toes to meet the ball correctly. The backlift will need rather more room than the back defensive shot, but otherwise the two are similar. The bat must be brought down straight, but instead of blocking the ball, it must be forced through its line, by the firm bottom hand on the handle.

To play the shot effectively you'll have to keep your elbows bent slightly and your head must stay forward and down. The power of the shot comes from a little punch given by the wrists uncocking just before impact, but as with all attacking shots the follow through is essential in forcing the ball. In this case the bat face can either finish high, or else with the arms fully extended and the wrists turned over, with the power of the shot taking the bat over the left shoulder.

Off drive and on drive

When you are bowled a ball which is well pitched up on a line that is either on, or outside the off stump then you can play the off drive, one of the most satisfying cricket shots.

This is a forward shot, so you need to go through the basic movements of the forward defensive shot.

Start with your high backlift. Then pick up the line of the ball and put your front foot out alongside this so that you can put all your weight onto it.

Point your left shoulder along the line of the ball and keep your eye on the ball as it comes towards you. Keep the wrists cocked as you start to swing down with a straight bat and then uncock them just before the face of the bat hits the ball.

This will give the shot its extra power. Keep your head over the ball and the bat angled down just a little. Then go into your follow through with the bat swinging through the line of the ball. Let your wrists turn over as the bat swings up and let your weight move through as well so that you move up onto the toes of your back foot. The shot finishes with the bat over your left shoulder and with your chest pointing along the line of the ball.

The on drive is almost exactly the same except that the body is squarer to the line of the ball. Play this shot to balls pitching on, or outside a line on the leg stump. Step out with your front foot beside the line of the ball and then follow through the motions given for the off drive, making sure as always that you swing right through the line of the ball to the end of the follow through.

Cut off the back foot

One of the most enjoyable ways of punishing a bad ball is to play a cut off the back foot. The most common of these is the **square cut**. This is a shot played to a short ball, which pitches wide of the off stump, and which is usually bowled by a fairly fast bowler.

The batsman playing a cut off the back foot should aim to send the ball either side of the fielder standing at **point**. In other words he should aim to send it at right angles to the pitch.

As soon as you spot the bad ball coming towards you, move your right leg back across the wicket to give yourself room. You want to be in a position to hit the ball when it comes alongside your right leg, with your arms fully stretched.

So from the backlift you must bring the face of the bat down onto the ball just as it comes into line with your back leg and your back foot, which will be pointing in the direction in which you are aiming the shot.

Place your weight on your right leg to give extra drive to the shot and bring your bat down smoothly on top of the ball. The bat has to come down to avoid sending the ball up in the air and giving away a catch to the slips.

Pulling a ball

The pull shot is really a controlled version of the sort of shot that you might play when you first start playing cricket — the sort of stroke that you are told that you should never play. While it's perfectly true that the pull and other cross bat shots (ones in which the bat is at right angles to the straight bat) must not be played to well bowled deliveries, the pull is a good shot to play against certain bad balls.

The sort of ball which is well suited to the pull is the very short one, which pitches on a line with the wicket, or the off stump. Though it must never be played to the ball moving as a result of any spin. Very short deliveries are easy targets because they give the batsman plenty of time to see how fast, at what height and in what direction the ball is coming towards him. This means that he can play a cross bat shot, like the pull, with a fair chance of hitting it well.

You can pull a ball off the front foot, or off the back foot, although off the back foot is more usual. It gives that extra bit of time. Once you have seen the ball as a likely one to be pulled step back and give the bat a good backlift. Watch the ball carefully and swing the bat down in a semi-horizontal arc so that you hit the ball across the pitch to the leg side. You must keep the ball down though, to avoid giving a catch and to do this you need to roll your wrists over as you hit the ball.

Once you've mastered this shot you can learn to send many bad balls racing for four runs by steering them away from any fielders.

Hitting the full-pitch to leg

A full-pitched ball coming down the leg side always looks like a perfect target to the batsman, yet it's amazing how often this shot is missed through batsmen not concentrating on the ball, or trying to hit it too hard.

In hitting a full-pitch on the leg side it is vital to get your head into the correct position before anything else. Your head will lead your body and will therefore govern the whole shot. What you want to aim for is a position where your head is over the line of the ball and looking along its line of flight. But don't let it move from that point until after you have finished the stroke. If you do, you will miss the shot.

You'll have to move forward as well, so your front foot will move out to the line of the ball and will end up pointing down the pitch. This leg will bear all your weight when you actually hit the ball so you will have to be comfortably balanced.

To play the shot accurately you must get onto the line of the ball quickly and play the stroke so that you hit the ball in front of your front leg when your arms are fully stretched. If your elbows are bent, you can't hit the ball properly. So, as with the pull, you need to sweep the bat face down in an arc from the backlift and then roll the wrists as you hit the ball, to keep it down.

Good balance and timing are important in this shot, but executed well it will really punish a bad ball.

Late cut

The late cut is one of the most enjoyable shots to see a bats-man play. He uses all his skill and timing to nudge the ball on its way, instead of hitting it in the other direction. However, it is a shot which calls for a cool head and great concentration.

The type of ball suited to a late cut is one similar to that which would be hit by a square cut. The only difference being that this ball is pitched shorter than the one hit with a square cut. But as with other balls that turn, don't try to use it against an off spinner, or a ball swinging in towards you.

The preparation is similar to all cuts off the back foot. Move back and place your foot in the direction where you intend to hit the ball. Balance your weight on your back leg. Cock your wrists so that the bat is over your shoulder. Then play the shot by bringing your hands down to whip the ball away as it comes almost level with the stumps. The ball is hit quite low, and at the moment of impact, the wrists must be rolled over to keep it on the ground. As the ball flies away, the bat continues to roll and swing across the body to complete the follow through.

If done correctly the ball should pass just wide of the slips.

Long hop hit to leg

Balls pitched short and wide of the leg stump are a delight to hit to the boundary. But like every ball, bad as well as good, they have to be hit with care.

However, this is an easy stroke to master as long as you follow the simple rules. First and most importantly, this shot must only be played to balls that pitch outside the leg stump. If a ball is straight it must be played with a straight bat.

To get into position for the shot move your back foot back and across the wicket until it is just outside the off stump. Then move your front foot so that it is in line with the flight of the ball and level with the back foot.

This will leave you standing square to the pitch. Raise your bat high on the backlift and try to swing it horizontally with your arms at full stretch, so that you hit the ball along a line that runs in front of square leg. Keep it down by rolling your wrists as you hit it and don't turn your head round while you are making the stroke, this could well send the ball straight to the man fielding at square leg. Try instead to make your eyes follow the ball as it flies away from the bat.

Hooking the high ball

The hook is one of the most difficult shots a batsman has to learn, mainly because it is used to hit fast bouncers coming anywhere between knee height and head height.

Any ball which pitches very short and is bowled on a line with the middle or leg stumps can be hit with a hook. But the batsman has to know exactly what he is doing as he has very little time to get into position and hit the ball.

The shot is really the same as the pull, except that it is played higher. To play it the batsman should go back on his right leg with all his weight balanced on it. He should try to have his leg and more importantly his head outside the line of the ball, so that if he does miss the ball, the ball will also miss him.

To hit a high ball like this you'll need a very high backlift, because even this ball will need to be kept down, to be absolutely safe — and that means swinging the bat down onto it.

You have to try to swing the bat in a horizontal arc, so that it is at right angles to the ground when you hit the ball.

You should aim to hit the ball between square leg and mid wicket and, as with other shots like this, you'll avoid giving catches if you roll your wrists as you hit the ball.

But if you want a really big hit and reckon that you can time it just right, aim to hit the ball up and it should sail over the boundary for a splendid six.

DEFENSIVE PLAY

This is a game for five players which gives batsmen practice in playing the basic forward and back defensive shots with a straight bat.

To play the game you need a bat, a ball, a wicket, and, if you are playing on a hard surface, three chalk lines drawn straight down the pitch from the base of the **stumps**. These help the batsman judge his aim and they help the bowler pitch the ball on target.

One player begins as the batsman, another as wicket-keeper, a third as the bowler, and the other two as a slip and another close fielder.

The bowler stands about three metres from the batsman and pitches the ball with a throw, for greater accuracy. He has to try to pitch balls of good line and length on the three lines on the ground. But every other ball he must pitch short, forcing the batsman to play a back defensive shot. So the bowler's rhythm is one ball well pitched up, one ball short, one ball well pitched up, etc.

> The batsman has an innings of two overs (12 balls). He must play defensive shots to every ball both forward and back. For every ball he keeps on the ground he gets a run. He loses a run if he misses a ball, or if he hits it like an attacking shot. He loses his whole score if he gives a catch or is bowled. But he wins a run if he is **bowled** a ball that is not accurate.

After each innings the players change roles. The one with the highest score at the end wins.

BOWLING

The bowler is the cutting edge of his side's attack. If he bowls well he both prevents the batsman from scoring runs and he forces them to make mistakes which get them out. But good bowling requires as much concentration as good batting.

First class bowlers may often bowl for hours on end, with only a few minutes rest between each over. Yet they have to keep up a constant pressure on the batsmen. As soon as a bowler begins to tire and lose his line and length, then the batsmen can take advantage of this and start to score off his bowling.

> So bowlers, especially fast bowlers, have to be fit as well as determined.

Even if a bowler does not make many wickets himself, he can be of great use to his side by pinning down the batsmen with good, accurate bowling, which prevents them from scoring runs. If he can persevere like this, the batsmen will begin to tire themselves. Then the bowler can take his opportunity and force them to make mistakes.

The way in which you hold the ball is called the **grip**. Your grip governs the way the ball moves after you have bowled it. Grips differ according to the type of ball you want to bowl, but the standard grip is with the seam vertical, your thumb underneath it and your first two fingers on top at either side. Your other fingers fit round the bottom side and join your thumb.

Bowling action

Bowling requires an action which is quite different from throwing. When you throw a ball you bend your elbow. If you bend your elbow when you are bowling this is illegal and the umpire will call **No Ball**. This gives a run to the other side.

So bowling has an action which you have to learn. At first it may feel unnatural, but with practice it will become relaxed and fluid.

Before you start to take a very long run and try to be a fast bowler, you must learn the correct action. Bear in mind that cricket is a sideways game, so that just as with batting, when you bowl you have to point your leading shoulder down the pitch towards the batsman. If you are a right-handed bowler it is your left shoulder, if you are left-handed, it is your right shoulder.

Your bowling arm needs to be kept as straight and as high as possible during your bowling action. Your head needs to be kept still and as you approach the wicket you can keep your eyes fixed on the stumps at the far end by looking to the outside of your leading arm.

Try to keep this front arm up high as well, it will help you change your weight from the back foot to the front foot as you bowl.

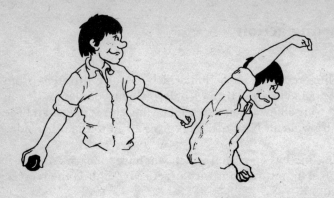

Your front arm will come down, like one half of a see-saw, and your bowling arm will come up like the other. When your bowling arm is at its highest, that's the time to let go of the ball.

Run and follow through

Before you even start to introduce a run into your action, practise standing still, holding a ball in your bowling hand and going through the circular motion of the action with your arms. Feel your weight move from the back foot to the front, just as you raise your bowling arm to its highest point. Finally, keep your eyes fixed on your imaginary wicket after you have released the ball, never let your head drop as the ball is released.

Once you're happy with the action try it with a short run. The reason a bowler runs up to bowl is that this gives him the right momentum to bowl the ball at the pace he requires. You may find that you are best suited to bowling at a slow pace. If this is the case, don't try to give yourself unnecessary speed. Apart from anything else pounding up a long run to the wicket tires you out. It is no accident that the top class fast bowlers are all large, powerful men. They need to be to keep up their pace for over after over.

Anyway to begin with, start with a short run up, to get the feel of how to arrive at the wicket at the right point in your action. Start by running straight to the wicket, this makes it much easier to transfer your weight correctly.

The most important stride of your run up is the last one. This is the **delivery stride** into which you jump from your run. You have to be careful to get this right for two reasons. One to make your action smooth and flowing. The other to comply with the rule which governs where the bowler's feet must land when he bowls.

Dealing with this rule first; to be legal a bowling action must finish with the bowler's back foot behind, and inside the return crease − and with at least some part of his front foot behind the popping crease. If you break this rule a **No Ball** is called and the batsman can either score runs or his side be awarded an extra.

So bearing this in mind, it is important to pace out your run from the wicket so that you have just the right amount of space to fit in your run and still land with your feet correctly positioned.

Now go through the
motions of your run.

Start by approaching
the wicket square on.

At the last stride
before the delivery
stride jump off your
left foot (if you are
right-handed), and
start to turn your body
sideways to the wicket.
At this point your
leading arm should be
pointing upwards and
the ball should be held
alongside your face.

Now bring your right foot down, on or behind the return crease, with your leading shoulder pointing to the batsman — you are completely sideways on, looking past the outside of your raised arm.

From this position take your delivery stride by moving your left foot as straight as possible down the wicket and landing it on or behind the popping crease. As the left foot comes down, the bowling arm swings up in its arc and the leading arm swings down. The left leg should be braced to take all your weight as you swing your bowling arm up high and round, to release the ball as it swings through its highest point. Keep your bowling arm moving after you have delivered the ball and keep your eyes fixed on the wicket. Let your back foot come up as you follow through, but if you take another pace down the pitch remember not to drag your feet as this tears up the batting surface and makes you unpopular with every batsman, as well as with the umpire.

Make quite sure that you can bowl smoothly and comfortably before trying to add pace to your delivery. Never sacrifice a good bowling action for extra pace — it won't help you take any more wickets.

Line and length

You'll hear people discussing **line and length** until they're blue in the face, but if you don't understand what they mean, they are wasting their time.

> The **line** of a delivery is the direction the ball takes down the pitch after it leaves the bowler's hand. A good line is generally one on which the ball will hit the wicket. The **length** of a delivery is the spot on the pitch where the ball bounces (if it does not bounce at all it is a **full-toss**). A good length is one which has the batsman confused and unable to make up his mind whether he should go forward or back to play it. The length of a delivery will depend on the pace at which it is bowled. A fast bowler will need to pitch his ball shorter for a good length, because of his extra pace, than a slow bowler.

There are no hard and fast rules about where a ball should bounce because the condition of different pitches will affect length. The behaviour of the batsmen is a surer guide. If they are worried by the bowling and forced to make mistakes that is all that matters.

Anyone who can keep on bowling a good line and length under any conditions has a right to be called a good bowler, because he is flexible — and the secret to his skill is accuracy and judgement.

After a few balls, an experienced bowler should be able to work out how the pitch is responding to his bowling and adjust his length accordingly. But having made these adjustments he should aim to drop the ball on the same spot every time he wants to bowl a delivery of just the right length. So this is what you must practise.

There are two places that a bowler should try to hit with his delivery. One is the spot on the pitch where he wants the ball to bounce, the other is the stump he is aiming to hit. If he looks at the first, the other will automatically be in his sight at the same time.

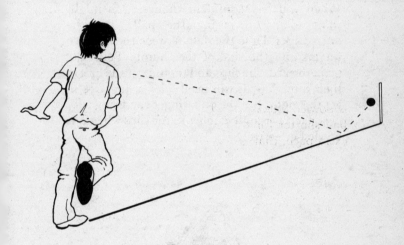

You can either learn to hit these two points by bowling at a single stump, or a mark on the wall, with a line stretching straight out along the ground down the pitch. Or else you can place a marker, like a piece of paper pinned in place, over the spot where you want the ball to bounce, and bowl at a normal wicket of three stumps.

Whichever you decide on, the practice you put in will be well rewarded by accurate bowling. But if you cut corners and don't learn how to bowl accurately, you'll never be given a chance to bowl in a match.

Swing bowling

Once you've learned how to bowl a good line and length, you will probably want to add a little variety to your bowling. If you want to add pace, build up gradually, keeping accuracy as you get faster — and not getting faster until you are accurate again.

When you feel confident though, you might want to try to swing the ball. Try the **outswinger**. Hold the ball between the first two fingers and the side of the thumb. Point the seam towards the slips and try to steer the ball in their direction. It will need a lot of practice to get this right, but the outswinger can bring a lot of wickets through catches to the slips when it is bowled effectively.

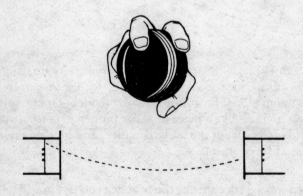

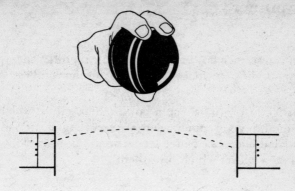

The **inswinger** is easier. Hold the ball between the first two fingers and the side of the thumb, well out of the palm of your hand. As you bowl stamp your foot down towards the batsman and steer the ball towards him.

Off spinner

When you start to bowl for the first time try different types of bowling at different paces to see which suits you best.

In particular try to be a spin bowler. This requires skill and cunning, but good spin bowlers are very sought after and the really good ones, like Derek Underwood for example, can be lethal on a wicket which suits them.

The spin bowler's run to the wicket is like that of the faster bowlers except that he runs less far and less fast. When you arrive at the wicket, try to place your front foot in front of the stumps and swivel on it.

To bowl an off spinner you need to grip the ball tight around the seam with the top joints of your fingers. Squeeze the ball between your first three fingers as hard as you can.

Then as you deliver the ball turn your wrist as if you were winding a clock. This will give the ball its spin.

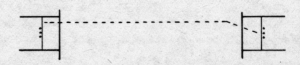

Leg spinner

The approach to the wicket is similar to that for bowling an off spinner. But for the leg spinner you must grip the ball between the knuckles of the first and third fingers tight around the seam. Then when you deliver the ball, turn your wrist in the opposite direction to that in which you turn it for an off spinner. This will obviously make the ball spin the other way.

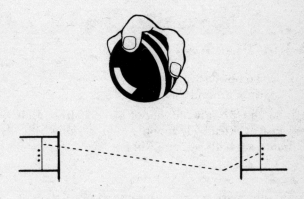

Any spin bowling takes a lot of practice. Apart from the skill of actually making the ball turn, you will have to learn how to judge the correct line of the ball, so that it bounces outside the line of the wicket and then comes into the batsman. You will have to make sure too that you always bowl a good length. If you bowl a slow delivery short, no matter how much spin you have on the ball, the batsman will always have plenty of time to see it coming, and if he's any good he will hit it for four runs with no difficulty.

However, once you have confidence to deliver a well pitched up slow ball with a good amount of spin, it can become very satisfying. What's more, in a side top-heavy with pace bowlers, you'll be very useful and will get a lot of bowling, which will help you improve even more.

Bowling Practice

Here is a game for any number of players although it can be played just as effectively by only one. To play, ideally you should have six balls but one will do.

Set up a full-length pitch, with some sort of wicket at the far end in front of a wall, a net, or an old sheet hung up to stop the balls. Then mark two areas in front of the wicket, one over a good length for a fast delivery, the other over a good length for a slow delivery.

Now decide what pattern you will adopt in the over and bowl six deliveries to see if you can keep to it. For instance you may decide to bowl six off spinners. In this case you should try to bounce your ball on the same spot outside the off stump every time and hit the wicket after that. Or you might decide to bowl alternate leg spinners and faster deliveries.

If there are two or more players you can each try in turn to follow the same pattern.

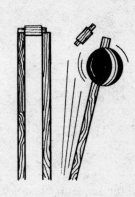

To score in the game you award yourself four points for hitting the marked area on the ground, two points for hitting the wicket and a bonus of six if you do this three times in a row.

However, if you fail to hit either the mark, or the wicket then you take off six from your score, because the batsman is assumed to have hit you for six.

As you get more accurate, try to make your bowling patterns more difficult and demanding. But to begin with be satisfied with just being able to bowl six balls in a row with good line and length.

Caught and bowled

This is a game which you can play all by yourself, but which will quicken your reflexes and improve your bowling skill. You will need to be able to play it up against a wall, or a garage door. If it is possible to have a full 22 yards (20.12 m) of level ground in front of this so much the better, but this is not essential.

The idea of the game is to bowl spin deliveries to pitch on a good length and then bounce towards a target area, which can be made either from a sheet of paper, or if you can find one, a sheet of hardboard. Colour two squares on the target about the height of the top of a stump and about 15 cm square. These squares should be about 30 cm apart.

If you can bowl from a full 22 yards (20.12 m) away then bowl normal deliveries at the target. If this is impossible though, stand as far from the target as you can and throw the ball.

The object of the game is to deliver alternate off spinners and leg spinners that pitch in front of the target and then hit the square on the side opposite the one where they pitched. Apart from doing this, you have to follow up the delivery by running down the pitch and catching the ball as it bounces back off the wall and before it hits the ground.

If you miss the target but catch the ball score four runs against you. If you miss both score six against you. The aim is to bowl a maiden over, losing no runs. See how low you get.

WICKET-KEEPING

Wicket-keepers are always at the centre of attention of any match, so they have to concentrate very hard all the time. When the ball is being bowled they have to watch to see which way it is moving, to be able to stop it behind the stumps if the batsman misses it. They have to be on the look out too for the chance of a catch, or a **stumping**, if the batsman makes a mistake. And if the batsman runs and the ball has not gone over the boundary, the wicket-keeper has to get into position right behind the stumps to catch the ball thrown in to the wicket by the fielder who retrieves it. So wicket-keeping is exciting, but it is also demanding both on your body and on your mind.

Wicket-keepers, like batsman, are in the direct line of the ball when it is bowled, so they have to be well protected from fast deliveries. Wicket-keepers wear pads on their legs, they wear special protectors in their groins and heavy, padded gloves on their hands. All these have to be comfortable, because they will be worn for hours on end and often in a crouching position.

The gloves are the most important pieces of a wicket-keeper's equipment. At first they will feel terribly heavy and inflexible. So you must bend them until they fit your hands comfortably — if you don't you will drop catches. You must have confidence in the gloves too. No matter how hard the ball and no matter how fast it may be coming at you, if you catch it properly, the gloves will absorb all the impact and it won't hurt you at all.

Stance and catching

The wicket-keeper is really a close fielder. This means that like the slips and other close fielders he has to be in a position to move in any direction very quickly. In order to do this, therefore, he must crouch near the ground when the bowler comes up to bowl.

The wicket-keeper's stance is special though. He should squat down with his feet slightly apart and his weight evenly balanced on the balls of his feet. His knees should be bent outwards so that his hands can hang down in front of and between his feet, with the gloves close together to form a catching cup. (Some wicket-keepers cross their little fingers to make their catching cup stronger when stopping hard balls).

79

This anyway is the basic stance for a wicket-keeper. From this position he can move quickly to one side or the other to take a catch, or stop a wide ball. He can also spring into the air to take a high catch or stop an unexpected bouncer.

The first thing that you must learn as a wicket-keeper is how to catch the ball correctly and consistently. Hold your hands together with the fingers pointing down. Watch the ball all the way from the bowler's hand. Even if you do not actually catch the ball, because the batsman hits it, you should expect every ball to come to you and move your hands to the stumps accordingly, because stumping should be second nature to you.

Where to stand

Clearly the position of the wicket-keeper relative to the wicket will depend on the type of bowling that he has to cope with.

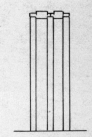

You should stand back behind the stumps for a quick bowler, so that you can take the ball comfortably at waist height. You'll have to judge for yourself how far back you do stand, but don't go further away from the wicket than you really need to.

For a slow bowler you will need to be close behind the wicket, perched just behind the off stump, so that you can see the ball coming. The ball will not be travelling fast enough to make taking it difficult, but if you are standing right up to the stumps you might have a chance to stump the batsman who moves down the wicket to drive a slow ball and misses.

In both cases, a wicket-keeper must have good vision. He must be ready too for the sudden chance which comes when a batsman snicks a ball off the edge of his bat. Nothing may have happened for several overs and then this opportunity to take a wicket presents itself in a fraction of a second. The wicket-keeper who misses it is very unpopular. The one who makes the catch can often alter the course of a match.

Taking a ball on the leg side

Balls that come down the leg side should be taken in the same way as balls coming down the off side. They are made slightly more difficult however, because the wicket-keeper has to move much further behind the wicket from his position outside the off stump.

Straight balls and those outside the off stump require the wicket-keeper to move his outside foot out so that he can get his head and body over the line of the ball.

Ones coming down the leg side obviously require a movement in the opposite direction. Quite often the wicket-keeper will have to take more than one sideways step.

To do this he must move rather like a crab, taking one step with his inside leg, then bringing the outside leg up to join it and then taking a second step with the inside leg, and so on until he is in line with the ball. In reality this happens like a series of hops as the wicket-keeper moves quickly and easily across the wicket to gather the ball.

Whether he is taking a ball on the off side, or on the leg side, the wicket-keeper should always keep his hands low and then bring them up with the bounce of the ball. He should never snatch at the ball, but wait for it to come into his gloves, giving with his arms in the direction in which the ball is travelling.

Even if he is taking a ball on the leg side though, the wicket-keeper should be in a position to carry out a quick stumping if he has the opportunity. So he must practise gathering the ball and moving it towards the bails in one movement.

Taking a rising ball

Taking a rising ball is really a case of watching the ball carefully and judging how high it is going to be when it reaches your gloves.

The wicket-keeper should stand up with his eyes on the ball as he sees it bounce off the pitch and move his gloves into position with the fingers pointing down to take the ball.

With very high balls though, and with catches that come from above he will have to alter the position of his gloves. Instead of pointing down, the fingers must point up.

The palms must be held open towards the ball, so that the hands can close round it as soon as it is safely in their grasp. This will enable the wicket-keeper to watch the ball through his hands as it comes towards him. His arms must give with the ball as they would with any other catch, to absorb its impact and stop the ball from bouncing out of his grasp.

BEING OUT

Stumped

There are nine ways in which a batsman can be out, being **stumped** is one of them.

A batsman can be stumped if he has no part of his body, or his bat behind the popping crease (in other words between the popping crease and the wicket). This can happen if he has moved down the wicket to hit a ball and has completely missed it. The force of his stroke still carries the batsman forward, while the ball shoots past him to the gloves of the waiting wicket-keeper. If the wicket-keeper can quickly knock off the bails before the batsman gets his bat, or some part of his body back behind the popping crease then the batsman will be out.

The wicket-keeper must break the wicket with the hand in which he is holding the ball. He is only allowed to take the ball from behind the wicket – which is usually the case anyway. However, if the batsman has hit the ball, or hit the wicket-keeper, then the wicket-keeper is allowed to take the ball from in front of the wicket and use it to stump the batsman, if he is outside the popping crease.

Run out

A wicket-keeper is often responsible for a **run out**, which is a very similar type of dismissal to a stumping.

A run out occurs when the batsmen are trying to take a run. If they have crossed and the wicket towards which one of them is running is broken before he can place his bat, or some part of his body over the popping crease, then he is out. If however, they have not crossed and the wicket from which one of them has run is broken then that batsman is out.

Run outs usually occur through bad running and good fielding. The general understanding on running is this. If the ball is hit in front of the striker's wicket, the decision whether to run or not is up to him. If the ball goes behind the wicket, whether he has hit it or not, the decision is up to the back-up batsman at the other end, who has a much better view of the ball and the fielders moving in on it. Either batsman can send his fellow back if he is really in doubt, but this is more likely to cause a run out than running when you are told to. The back up batsman should help the striker by walking down the pitch as the bowler delivers the ball, this will give him a start on a run if the striker wants to take a quick single.

To avoid any doubt about run outs it is usual for batsmen to slide the toes of their bats along the ground at full arm stretch as they near the popping crease. If they do this they may be safely over the crease before any part of their body crosses the line.

Caught

A batsman can be **caught** out if any fielder (including the bowler and wicket-keeper) catches the ball after he has hit it with his bat, or after the ball has hit the batsman's hand or glove. If it hits his wrist he is not out. The ball of course must not have touched the ground between the hit and the catch.

There is one condition in which a clean catch does not dismiss a batsman though. This is the rare time when a fielder on the boundary catches the ball from a high hit **but steps outside the boundary either as he makes the catch, or immediately after he makes it**. When this happens a batsman can breathe a sigh of relief and make a note not to sky any more boundaries unless they sail high over for six runs, well out of the fielders' reach.

When a bowler catches the ball incidentally, this is referred to as being **caught and bowled** in the score book.

Bowled and hit wicket

A batsman is said to have been **bowled** when the ball delivered by the bowler breaks the wicket, in other words completely removes one or both bails from the top of the wicket. Even if the ball has hit the batsman or his bat, if it carries on to break the wicket, then he is said to have been bowled.

The bowler is also credited with a dismissal if the batsman breaks his own wicket while he is trying to play a delivery. This method of being out is called **hit wicket**. To avoid wasting your wicket in this way, you must keep a watchful eye on how far you step back to play short balls. You must watch your balance too.

Nothing would be worse than to hit a magnificent hook for six and then lose your balance completely and fall across your own wicket. It would be painful as well as a terrible waste.

Leg before wicket or l.b.w.

No other way of being out is open to so much argument and disagreement as **l.b.w.**, though fortunately the decision of the umpire is final – although it is not uncommon for a batsman to have a very different opinion about his verdict if he has given him out, or for fielders to feel cheated if he has given the batsman not out.

The problems arise in deciding what the ball would have done had it continued in its projected direction, because in the case of l.b.w. the ball has to be stopped by some part of the batsman's body, or his clothing – (not the bat, or the hands holding it).

If in the umpire's opinion the ball bounced on a line with the stumps or on a line with the outside of the off stump and would then have carried to the wicket, had it not been stopped, the batsman must be given out.

If the batsman deliberately pads away a ball outside the off stump, which would have hit his wicket, then he is out l.b.w. as well, even if he touched it well outside the line of the stump. If however, the ball pitches outside the leg stump the batsman cannot be given out l.b.w. under any circumstances.

Of course the bowler, the wicket-keeper and even the close fielders will all leap into the air and cry *How's that*, if they think there is the slightest chance of an l.b.w., but the decision rests with the umpire alone. After all he is the only impartial person with a perfectly clear view.

Hit ball twice, handle ball and obstruction

There are three very uncommon ways of being out as well as those already mentioned.

If you handle the ball except when asked to by one of the fielding side you can be given out **handle ball**.

You can be out **hit ball twice**, if after stopping the ball, you then hit it a second time in order to try to score runs.

And if you deliberately get in the way of one of the fielders and hinder what he is trying to do, you can be given out for **obstruction**.

These three are so easily avoided though, that any batsman who gets himself out as a result of one of them, really has no excuse at all.

UMPIRES

Cricket matches are controlled by two umpires. They should be impartial, that is to say they should not favour the players of one side or the other.

On the field the umpires take up two separate positions. One stands at the striker's end square of the wicket to have a view of the wicket and the batsmen's feet at right angles. He usually stands in the square leg position. The other umpire stands at the bowling end, looking over the wicket directly down the pitch to the striker's wicket. At the end of an over, this umpire calls **Over** and the fielders change ends. But the umpires stay at their own ends until the end of an innings. They simply move to the wicket at the bowling end and then move away from it to square leg after the over at their end has finished.

During the course of play the umpires communicate the score with the scorers off the field by means of a series of signals. But their principal responsibility is to see that the rules of cricket are followed and to decide when a batsman is out if there is a dispute, as is often the case with appeals for l.b.w.. To show that a batsman is **out** an umpire raises one finger in the air, though in Australia he raises his whole arm.

Umpires can be either men or women, though in all first class games they are men by tradition. Many umpires are retired players who have brought their wide experience of the game to control the play of others.

Wide signal

If a bowler bowls a ball which in the umpire's opinion is so high or so wide of the wicket that the batsman standing on a normal guard cannot reach it then this is called a **wide**.

The umpire will then signal a wide to the scorers by extending his arms horizontally in a **T** shape. The scorers will then add one extra to the batting side's score.

No ball signal

An umpire may call **No ball** if he feels that a bowler delivers a ball with a throwing action. He can also call **No ball** if the bowler changes the side of the wicket from which he bowls without notifying the umpire.

If the bowler throws the ball at the striker's wicket, before bowling at him, even if he is trying to run him out, that is a no ball also.

A no ball will be called too if the bowler's feet are in the wrong place when he bowls. His front foot must be partly on or totally behind the popping crease, while his back foot must not touch or land outside the return crease.

The signal for a no ball is one arm raised horizontally.

Signals for boundaries

When a batsman hits a ball which runs over the boundary after bouncing he is awarded **four runs** and the umpire signals this to the scorer by waving one arm from side to side to side.

When the ball passes over the boundary without touching the ground after it leaves the bat this is a **six**. The batsman is awarded six runs and the umpire signals this to the scorer by raising both arms into the air.

Signals for byes and leg byes

If the ball passes the striker after it has been bowled without touching him or his bat and the batsmen run successfully, the umpire signals to the scorer that these are extras called **byes**. To signal this he holds one open hand above his head.

If the ball hits the striker anywhere, except the hands holding the bat, and the batsmen run successfully, then these are regarded as **leg byes** and they are added to the score as such. The signal for a leg bye is given by the umpire by touching a raised knee.

If in either case the ball carries on to run over the boundary the umpire signals either four byes, or four leg byes, by giving the signal for a four, while either holding up one open hand (for byes) or touching a raised knee (for leg byes).

Signal for one off

If one or both batsmen do not run the full length of the pitch, from one popping crease to the other, while they are running between the wicket, then the umpire may signal **one off** after they have finished running, to indicate that one run must be deducted from the number that they ran.

The signal for one off is given by the umpire bending his arm up to touch his shoulder with the tips of his fingers.

SCORING

The basic ways in which you score in cricket have been mentioned earlier. However, there are a number of rules which govern circumstances when some runs are not counted. These really concern runs taken immediately before a batsman is dismissed.

If a batsman is caught out no runs are allowed, even if he has been able to make a run before the catch is taken.

If a batsman is run out, the run in question is not allowed, but any runs taken beforehand are.

In addition there are one or two occasions when a batsman can score more than six — though these are very rare.

If the batsmen succeed in running a greater number of runs before the ball crosses the boundary then that total, and not the total from the boundary itself is added to the score. In reality this would only ever occur with a very distant boundary when the ball ran for four runs, but the batsmen managed to run five or more runs.

In addition if a fielder throws the ball over the boundary as a result of an **overthrow** the batsmen's score will be increased by either four or six, depending on whether the overthrow hit the ground or not, before it went over the boundary. So if the batsmen had run three and the overthrow went for four runs, seven runs would be added to the score.

The score of a cricket match is kept by official scorers at the side of the field. They record the details of the individual batsmen's innings, their total scores, the number of boundaries they hit, the number of balls they received and the way in which they were out. And they also record details of the bowlers, the number of overs they bowled, the number of maiden overs they bowled, the number of wickets they took and the number of runs that were scored off them. The scorers also record the extras awarded by the umpires as well as keeping the score board up-to-date, if there is one.

This is what a score card looks like:

Test No. 818/49

FROM: WISDEN

NEW ZEALAND v ENGLAND 1977 - 78 (2nd Test)

Played at Lancaster Park, Christchurch, on 24, 25, 26, 28 February, 1 March.
Toss: England.   Result: ENGLAND won by 174 runs.
Debuts: England – C.T. Radley.

Botham became the second England player after A.W. Greig (*Test No. 733*) to score a hundred and take five wickets in an innings of the same Test.

ENGLAND

B.C. Rose	c Howarth b Chatfield	11	c Lees b Collinge	7
G. Boycott*	lbw b Collinge	8	run out	26
D.W. Randall	c Burgess b Hadlee	0	run out	13
G.R.J. Roope	c Burgess b Hadlee	50	(6) not out	9
G. Miller	c Congdon b Collinge	89		
C.T. Radley	c Lees b Hadlee	15		
I.T. Botham	c Lees b Boock	103	(4) not out	30
R.W. Taylor†	run out	45		
C.M. Old	b Hadlee	8	(5) b Collinge	1
P.H. Edmonds	c Lees b Collinge	50		
R.G.D. Willis	not out	6		
Extras	(B 14, LB 9, NB 10)	33	(B 4, LB 3, NB 3)	10
Total		418	(4 wickets declared)	96

NEW ZEALAND

J.G. Wright	c and b Edmonds	4	c Roope b Willis	0
R.W. Anderson	b Edmonds	62	b Willis	15
G.P. Howarth	c Edmonds b Willis	5	c Edmonds b Old	1
M.G. Burgess*	c Roope b Botham	29	not out	6
B.E. Congdon	lbw b Botham	20	c Botham b Willis	0
J.M. Parker	not out	53	c Botham b Edmonds	16
W.K. Lees†	c Miller b Botham	0	b Willis	0
R.J. Hadlee	b Edmonds	1	c Botham b Edmonds	39
R.O. Collinge	c Edmonds b Botham	32	c Miller b Botham	0
S.L. Boock	c Taylor b Edmonds	2	c Taylor b Botham	0
E.J. Chatfield	c Edmonds b Botham	3	lbw b Botham	6
Extras	(B 4, LB 1, NB 19)	24	(LB 6, NB 16)	22
Total		235		105

NEW ZEALAND	O	M	R	W	O	M	R	W		FALL OF WICKETS			
										E	NZ	E	NZ
Hadlee	43	10	147	4	6	1	17	0					
Collinge	26.5	6	89	3	9	2	29	2	*Wkt*	*1st*	*1st*	*2nd*	*2nd*
Chatfield	37	8	94	1	5	0	22	0	1st	15	37	25	2
Congdon	18	11	14	0	2	0	18	0	2nd	18	52	47	14
Boock	21	11	41	1					3rd	26	82	67	19
									4th	127	119	74	25
ENGLAND									5th	128	148	–	25
Willis	20	5	45	1	7	2	14	4	6th	288	151	–	59
Old	14	4	55	0	7	4	9	1	7th	294	153	–	81
Botham	24.7	6	73	5	7	1	38	3	8th	305	211	–	90
Edmonds	34	11	8	4	6	2	22	2	9th	375	216	–	95
									10th	418	235	–	105

Umpires: F.R. Goodall and R.L. Monteith.

GREAT CRICKETERS

Natural talent obviously helps a great deal when it comes to creating great cricketers, but it is interesting how many of the top bowlers started their cricketing careers as batsmen perhaps, or as different sorts of bowlers, and how many top class batsmen began as indifferent fielders and have forced themselves to become far better fielders in order to improve their own game. There is a simple lesson to be learned from every top class player. Natural talent helps, but natural talent without practice and a determination to become even better gets you nowhere.

All the great cricketers had to start somewhere, many of them had less formal coaching than a lot of cricketers get today at school. But they made good use of the lessons they did learn and they were never too good to keep on learning.

One of the most famous cricketers of all time was an Australian — the legendary **Don Bradman**. When he was a boy, Bradman used to practise for hours with just a stump and a wall. But from these quiet beginnings he grew into a batsman who scored 29 hundreds in Test matches, more Test centuries than any other batsman. When he retired in 1949 Don Bradman had scored a total of 20,067 runs and his average stood at an amazing figure of over 95 runs for every innings. When he played in England in 1938 he averaged more than 115 runs every time he batted.

Bradman's amazing record stands on its own, but the Yorkshire batsman, **Geoff Boycott** has twice averaged over 100 runs per innings during the season. However, the batsman with more runs to his name than any other in a single season was **Denis Compton**.

In 1947 Denis scored 3816 runs for Middlesex and England. He hit 18 centuries that season and as a result became one of the few batsmen ever to hit a hundred hundreds. The first of this memorable band was the great Dr. W.G. Grace.

W.G. Grace was one of the founders of modern cricket. He was a huge man with a long beard, and his face has become as famous in cricketing circles as that of any other sportsman in any other sport. His beard was particularly famous, one Australian bowler named Jones is even said to have once bowled a ball straight through it! But aside from being a great cricketing character, Grace was a fine bowler and an even better batsman who knew all the batting techniques long before modern experts were telling us how to play. In fact he was so respected among his fellow players that he was known as **The Champion**.

However, W.G. Grace does not hold the record for the most centuries scored in a career. That record belongs to a later cricketer, 'The Master', **Jack Hobbs**. Like Don Bradman, Garfield Sobers and Len Hutton, Jack Hobbs was knighted for his services to cricket and became Sir Jack Hobbs. He used to open the batting for both his county, Surrey, and for England. During his outstanding career he scored no less than 197 centuries.

It was while Jack Hobbs was playing for Surrey that the fastest century ever was scored, though Hobbs did not hit it himself. That honour belongs to his captain **Percy Fender**, who scored a hundred runs in 35 minutes in a match against Northamptonshire in 1920.

There have been other fast scores over the years too. In 1903 **Gilbert Jessop**, nicknamed 'The Croucher', hit 200 runs in two hours, and seventy-three years later, in 1976, Clive Lloyd, the West Indies captain, did exactly the same thing when playing for Lancashire against Glamorgan. But even these remarkable scores cannot compare with that of Edwin Alleston of Nottinghamshire, who scored 189 runs in only 90 minutes in a match against Sussex in 1911.

There has only been one occasion in the history of recorded cricket in which a batsman has hit a six off every ball of an over. This happened in 1968 when **Garry** (now Sir Garfield) **Sobers** hit six sixes off an over bowled by Malcolm Nash.

At the time Sobers was captain of Northamptonshire and the ball that he hit for thirty-six runs in that over is now in the county museum.

Sobers was also a great bowler and fielder. In fact he is regarded as one of the greatest all-round cricketers that there has ever been. As well as his six sixes he also holds the record for the highest innings in a Test match, 365 not out for the West Indies scored against Pakistan. The previous record was held by **Len Hutton**, who scored 364 for England against Australia in 1938.

But batsmen don't always have it their own way. In 1877 the Oxford University side were all bowled out for a total of 12 by the M.C.C.. And thirty years later Northamptonshire were all bowled out for same score by Gloucestershire. The lowest score ever made by a batting side in a Test match was the sorry figure of 26, scored by New Zealand against England in 1955.

So much for batsmen − bowlers have set a few memorable records of their own.

The bowler with the greatest number of wickets to his credit was **Wilfred Rhodes**, who took 4187 wickets in a career which ran from 1898 to 1930. In 1926 he was recalled to the England side at the ripe old age of 48, although he actually played his last game for England when he was 52 years old, only thirteen years off retiring age! As a young man Rhodes also opened the batting for England and understandably he was one of the greatest cricketers that his county, Yorkshire, has ever produced.

Rhodes was succeeded in the Yorkshire side by another left arm slow bowler, **Hedley Verity**. Verity once took all ten wickets in an innings whilst only ten runs were scored off his bowling. So he ended that innings with the amazing figures of ten for ten.

The bowler who took the most wickets in a season was **'Tich' Freeman** of Kent. He was another spin bowler who took 304 wickets in the 1928 season.

Yet another spin bowler holds the record for the most wickets taken in a match. In 1956, **Jim Laker** of Surrey bowled for England in the Test match against Australia at Manchester. He took 9 wickets in the first innings and all 10 wickets in the second innings — a total of 19 wickets in a match.

Although slow bowlers hold most of the records, great fast bowlers have been all important in winning matches for their sides. When England won the **Ashes**, by beating Australia in the 1933 Test series, the English bowler **Harold Larwood** took 33 wickets in the five matches.

Australia produced two great fast bowlers after the Second World War, Ray Lindwall and Keith Miller both made a name for themselves in 1948. Then it was the turn of English fast bowlers like 'Fiery' **Fred Trueman**, **Brain Statham** and 'Typhoon' **Frank Tyson** to steal the limelight. Today England's leading fast bowler is Warwickshire's **Bob Willis**. But against him the Australians can match **Dennis Lillee**, **Jeff Thomson** and **Rodney Hogg**, who took 41 wickets against England in the 1978−79 Test series. Thomson and Lillee are two of the fast bowlers of all time.

Like Australia, the West Indies has been a home of great fast bowlers since **Sir Learie Constantine** in the 1930's. The Caribbean islands, which form the West Indies, have produced fast bowlers like **Wes Hall**, **Charlie Griffith** and the modern generation of **Michael Holding**, **Wayne Daniel**, **Andy Roberts** and **Joel Garner**.

A fast bowler sending the wicket flying, and occasionally even breaking a stump, a great batsman scoring a century, a great wicket-keeper taking a seemingly impossible catch and a fine fielder sending back perfect throws time after time are all sights which make any cricketer eager to improve his own game. But it's worth remembering for a minute that all these great players were once inexperienced boys who had to learn through hours and hours of practice. Perhaps their secret to success lay in being able to appreciate the things they were learning and were teaching themselves. Practice, real practice is never boring in itself. If other cricketers tell you that it is, it's more likely that they have let it become boring themselves by not trying as hard as they can, and by not driving themselves to achieve that measure of perfection that might one day make them international players.

Who knows, if you do have that determined streak, you might appear in the England batting order one day.

THE LANGUAGE OF CRICKET

The Ashes

This is the imaginary trophy claimed by whichever side wins an England-Australia Test series. The name originated in 1882 when England was defeated by Australia for the first time. A newspaper report on the match referred to the death of English cricket and said that its **ashes** would be taken to Australia.

When England beat Australia in Melbourne though, in the next series, a small urn was presented to the English captain with **The Ashes** written on it. Inside were the ashes of a burnt stump. The urn is kept at Lord's today, but the series between the two countries is still known as the Ashes.

Beamer

A full-pitched ball which is aimed at the batsman's head to frighten him and cause him to make mistakes is known as a **beamer**. These are bowled by fast bowlers.

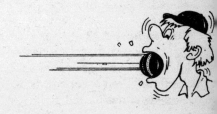

107

Bouncer

Like a beamer, a **bouncer** is bowled by a fast bowler to scare a batsman. As its name suggests a bouncer bounces off the pitch and flies up towards the batsman, often at head height. In order to make it do this a bowler must pitch the ball very short. If he does this too often though the umpire can warn him against bowling any more bouncers.

Bumper

A **bumper** is another name for a bouncer.

Carry one's bat

A batsman who is not out when his side's innings comes to an end is said to have **carried his bat**. The expression is usually applied to a batsman who also opened the innings. In other words he is one who has batted right through an innings and is not out at the end.

Chinaman

When a left-arm spinner bowls to a right-handed batsman he usually turns the ball away from him. When he bowls a **chinaman** though, he turns the ball the other way and throws the batsman off his guard.

Chop

A stroke played on the off-side by bringing the bat down hard on the ball as it passes the batsman is called a **chop**.

Cow shot

When a batsman hits across the line of a ball's flight and tries to hit the ball towards square leg or mid-wicket, this is known as a **cow-shot**. Cow-shots are usually played by mistake or as a result of a batsman losing his concentration and taking a wild sweep at the ball.

Daisy cutter

A ball that stays very
near to the ground
after it has pitched is
known as a **daisy
cutter**.

Dead ball

When the umpire decides that a ball has finally come to rest
in the hands of either the wicket-keeper or the bowler it
becomes a **dead ball**.

When the ball is dead
the batsmen are not
allowed to run, nor
can they be out, until
the bowler has bowled
his next delivery.

Declaring an innings

A captain may choose to end his side's innings before all the
batsmen have been out. When he does this he **declares his
innings** and the act of doing it is called a **declaration**.
Declarations are usually made when one side has made a high
score compared with the other, and the captain decides that
he has enough runs to win the game. By stopping his own
innings and putting the other side into bat he gives his side
longer to dismiss the other and so win the game outright.

Donkey drop

Slow balls that are bowled higher than usual so that they will fall on, or very close to, the wicket are called **donkey drops**.

They are usually easy targets for batsmen to hit.

Draw

In many games a draw occurs when both sides end the match with the same score. In cricket however, a **draw** is the result when a game ends before one side has completed its final innings. In matches that last for a set time, even in Test matches which last five days, you will often hear talk of one side playing for a draw.

This means that they have little chance of winning the game outright, but that they can avoid losing it provided that they can keep batting until the time runs out. In this case the batsmen have to play defensively to avoid being out, and the fielders have to attack hard to try to get them out.

Duck

This is not simply what you do when the ball sails over your head, parting your hair, as you stand at leg-slip. A **duck** describes a batsman's score when he is out having scored no runs. If he is out first ball that is a **golden duck**.

Flight

The **flight** of the ball is the path it follows through the air after it leaves the bowler's hand and before it pitches. A bowler will try to vary the flight of his deliveries to confuse the batsman.

Flipper

A leg-break bowler's ball with top-spin that comes to the bat at an irregular height after pitching is called a **flipper**.

Full toss

When a bowler bowls a delivery that does not pitch before it reaches the batsman it is called a **full toss**.

Gate

The area between the bat and the batsman's pad is called the **gate**. A batsman should never let a ball through the gate, and be bowled as a result.

Googly

A ball that looks to the batsman as if it has been bowled as a leg break but which in fact turns to the off is called a **googly**. In Australia they call a googly a **bosie**, or a **wrong 'un**.

Grub

This is another name for a daisy cutter.

Green wicket

A wicket with a good covering of grass is called a **green wicket**. Green wickets usually help fast bowlers and seam bowlers.

King pair

Batsmen who suffer the misfortune of being out twice first ball in a two innings match are said to have had a **king pair**.

Leg cutter

When a bowler bowls a ball which pitches on its seam and then changes its direction, because the seam bites into the pitch, this is called a cutter. A **leg cutter** turns into the wicket from the leg side. An **off-cutter** cuts in from the opposite side.

Long handle

The normal length of a handle on a cricket bat is about 30 cm. Taller players often use bats with **long handles** which are about 32 cm long. The overall length of a bat with a long handle is in the region of 88 cm.

Long hop

Short-pitched balls that hop easily to the batsmen and give him plenty of time to judge his shot and hit the ball well are called **long hops**.

Maiden over

If a bowler bowls an over off which the batsmen score no runs this is known as a **maiden over**.

Nelson

This peculiar term describes a score of exactly 111. The famous British sailor Admiral Horatio Nelson had only one eye and one arm. So a **Nelson** is all ones. A score of exactly 222 is a **Double Nelson**.

Nightwatchman

When a wicket falls near the end of a day's play a captain will often send a lower order batsman in to bat. This batsman who is promoted in the batting order is supposed to play out the time left for that day's play, so that the more experienced batsman, whose place he has taken, can come in to bat the following day, when there is less risk of his valuable wicket being lost at the end of a tiring day. The batsman who is promoted is therefore called a **nightwatchman**.

Overthrow

When a fielder returns a ball to the wicket, after fielding it, but his throw is so wild that the wicket-keeper, or other fielders can not stop it, this is called an **overthrow**. When there is an overthrow the batsmen are allowed to run, and if the ball goes over the boundary, either a six or a four is added to the striker's score, as well as the number of runs they have made off that ball before it crosses the boundary.

Pair

A batsman who fails to score in both innings of a match is said to have a **pair**. This is not quite as bad as a king pair, but it's bad enough.

Play on

A batsman can get himself if he plays a stroke which then carries to the wicket and breaks it. A snick or hit like this is said to be **played on**.

Plumb pitch/wicket

Batsmen like **plumb pitches** because the ball moves off them with regular pace and at a regular height. This makes batting much easier as shots are simpler to judge, and there is no chance of the ball suddenly doing something unexpected.

Polishing the ball

As a cricket ball becomes worn in the course of play, it loses its shine and its seam becomes worn down. While it is against the rules of cricket to pick at the seam to make it sharp again, it is permissible to **polish** the ball. The purpose of polishing the ball is help it to swing.

The way you polish it is to rub it against your flannels. Bowlers polish only one side of the ball, leaving the other side rough. This is because the shiny half will move through the air quicker than the rough half. So as the ball moves through the air the rough side catches it and the ball starts to spin. This movement helps the bowler to swing the ball one way or the other.

Popping crease

The **popping crease** takes its name from the **popping hole** which used to be part of the wicket in the early days of cricket. The popping hole used to be positioned between the two stumps and the batsman had to put his bat into it at the end of each run. But if the wicket-keeper could put the ball into the popping hole before the batsman got his bat there, then the batsman was out. But this arrangement was uncomfortable for wicket-keepers who often had their fingers hit by the bat coming into the hole, so the popping crease was developed. Today any batsman outside the popping crease can be stumped out.

Pop/pop up

Balls which rise sharply off the pitch after bouncing are said to **pop**, or **pop up**.

Runner

If a batsman is disabled and unable to run, but is still able to bat he may have a **runner** to run for him, provided that the captain of the fielding side agrees to this. The runner will be a member of the batsman's own team and he will stand at square-leg, when the disabled batsman has the strike and at the bowler's end at other times.

Set

This is an expression used to describe a batsman who has become well established in his innings and is able to score freely. He is therefore **set** in his innings.

Shine

Shine is put on the ball by the action of polishing it on the players' flannels.

Shooter

A ball which the batsman expects to rise but which stays low after it pitches is known as a shooter.

Short run

If a batsman does not ground his bat properly after running to a popping crease he is said to have run a **short run**. If this happens an umpire will signal **one off**.

Silly point/mid-on/mid-off

These are fielding positions very close to the bat in which the fielder often feels he is too close for his own good. They are positions in which quick catches can be taken.

Sticky wicket

This is a wicket which a batsman does not enjoy batting on. It is a wicket which dries quickly after being soaked with rain and on which the bowlers can make the ball break sharply and pop up unexpectedly, making batting very difficult.

Swing

The **swing** of a ball is the swerve it makes in flight. A bowler who makes a ball do this is said to make it **swing**.

Tail enders

The batsmen who bat last in a side's batting order are the tail enders. The tail enders are often players who are included in the side because of their bowling skill, rather than their skill with the bat.

Wicket maiden

An over in which a bowler takes one or more wickets and in which the batsmen score no runs is called a **wicket maiden**.

Yorker

A bowler can try to make a ball pitch under the batsman's bat as he moves forward to play his shot. If he does this it is known as a **yorker**, and if he succeeds the batsman is said to have been **yorked**. Yorkers have to be well pitched up in order to work. They are often described as pitching on the batsman's toes.

USEFUL ADDRESSES

United Kingdom: Test and County Cricket Board,
Lord's Ground,
St. John's Wood,
London NW8

Australia: Australian Cricket Board,
70 Jollimont Street,
Jollimont,
Victoria, 3002,
Australia

New Zealand: New Zealand Cricket Council,
P.O. Box 958,
Third Floor,
Simu Building,
Latimer Square,
Christchurch,
New Zealand

West Indies: West Indies Cricket Board of Control
9 Appleblossom Avenue,
Petit Valley,
Diego Martin,
Trinidad,
West Indies.

Canada: Canadian Cricketing Association,
574 Alpine Court,
North Vancouver,
British Columbia,
V7R 2L6,
Canada

U.S.A.: United States Cricketing Association,
7055 Purpleridge Drive,
Palos Verdes,
California, 90274,
U.S.A.

Ireland: Irish Cricket Union,
45 Foxrock Park,
Foxrock,
County Dublin,
Eire

YOU CAN SWIM with David Haller

Take a plunge into the dynamic sport of swimming with David Haller, former British team coach, and captain and competitor in the 1976 and 1980 Olympic games.

Whether learning to swim or improving your technique, whether you wish to swim for pleasure, competition, or simply survival, this comprehensive handbook takes you through gaining confidence in the water, developing the strokes, diving and fast, effective swimming for competitive racing, and includes games, exercises and advice from a great swimmer and top professional coach.

0 552 54197 4   85p

YOU CAN BE A GYMNAST with Avril Lennox

Join the thrilling world of modern gymnastics with Avril Lennox, MBE, former British Gymnastics Champion and now coach to the British Gymnastics Team.

Whether you wish to make a start or improve your performance in the gymnastics arena, you'll find everything you need to know in this superb handbook. First-rate information on how to begin, exercises for strength and flexibility, elementary work on the floor and apparatus, simple floor routines and plenty of tips and sound advice from an experienced gymnast at the very top of her field.

0 552 54198 5   85p

YOU CAN PLAY FOOTBALL with Gordon Banks

Make your name on the football field with Gordon Banks, top goalkeeper and member of the winning English World Cup Team.

Whether you're a newcomer to this demanding, fast-moving sport, or just looking to improve your game, this informative handbook will prove indispensable. Basic and advanced techniques, defensive and attacking ploys, games and exercises to develop specialised skills, and all the tactics of a match in action are expertly explained with helpful advice and personal tips from one of the greatest football figures in the world.

0 552 54200 8   85p

If you would like to receive a newsletter telling you about our new children's books, fill in the coupon with your name and address and send it to:

Gillian Osband,
Transworld Publishers Ltd,
Century House,
61–63 Uxbridge Road, Ealing,
London, W5 5SA

Name ....

Address ....

....

....

CHILDREN'S NEWSLETTER

All the books on the previous pages are available at your bookshop or can be ordered direct from Transworld Publishers Ltd., Cash Sales Dept., P.O. Box 11, Falmouth, Cornwall.

Please send full name and address together with cheque or postal order — no currency, and allow 40p per book to cover postage and packing (plus 18p each for additional copies).